My Dog's Medical Records

MW00436460

Dog's Name:

_____

Breed:

Gender:

Birthdate:

Weight:

Length:

Vet's Name:

Vet's Contact Info:

Vaccination Record

Date	Age	Vaccine	Brand	Batch #	Vet

Vaccination Record

Date	Age	Vaccine	Brand	Batch #	Vet

Vaccination Record

Date	Age	Vaccine	Brand	Batch #	Vet

Vaccination Record

Date	Age	Vaccine	Brand	Batch #	Vet

Vet Visit Log

Date   Time

Clinic:

Doctor Seen:

Reason For Visit:

Treatment Plan:

Medication:

Vaccinations:

Vet Visit Notes

Vet Visit Log

Date   Time

Clinic:

Doctor Seen:

Reason For Visit:

Treatment Plan:

Medication:

Vaccinations:

Vet Visit Notes

Vet Visit Log

Date   Time

Clinic:

Doctor Seen:

Reason For Visit:

Treatment Plan:

Medication:

Vaccinations:

Vet Visit Notes

Vet Visit Log

Date   Time

Clinic:

Doctor Seen:

Reason For Visit:

Treatment Plan:

Medication:

Vaccinations:

Vet Visit Notes

Vet Visit Log

Date   Time

Clinic:

Doctor Seen:

Reason For Visit:

Treatment Plan:

Medication:

Vaccinations:

Vet Visit Notes

Vet Visit Log

Date   Time

Clinic:

Doctor Seen:

Reason For Visit:

Treatment Plan:

Medication:

Vaccinations:

Vet Visit Notes

Vet Visit Log

Date   Time

Clinic:

Doctor Seen:

Reason For Visit:

Treatment Plan:

Medication:

Vaccinations:

Vet Visit Notes

Vet Visit Log

Date   Time

Clinic:

Doctor Seen:

Reason For Visit:

Treatment Plan:

Medication:

Vaccinations:

Vet Visit Notes

Vet Visit Log

Date   Time

Clinic:

Doctor Seen:

Reason For Visit:

Treatment Plan:

Medication:

Vaccinations:

Vet Visit Notes

Vet Visit Log

Date   Time

Clinic:

Doctor Seen:

Reason For Visit:

Treatment Plan:

Medication:

Vaccinations:

Vet Visit Notes

Vet Visit Log

Date   Time

Clinic:

Doctor Seen:

Reason For Visit:

Treatment Plan:

Medication:

Vaccinations:

Vet Visit Notes

Vet Visit Log

Date   Time

Clinic:

Doctor Seen:

Reason For Visit:

Treatment Plan:

Medication:

Vaccinations:

Vet Visit Notes

Vet Visit Log

Date   Time

Clinic:

Doctor Seen:

Reason For Visit:

Treatment Plan:

Medication:

Vaccinations:

Vet Visit Notes

Vet Visit Log

Date   Time

Clinic:

Doctor Seen:

Reason For Visit:

Treatment Plan:

Medication:

Vaccinations:

Vet Visit Notes

Vet Visit Log

Date   Time

Clinic:

Doctor Seen:

Reason For Visit:

Treatment Plan:

Medication:

Vaccinations:

Vet Visit Notes

Vet Visit Log

Date   Time

Clinic:

Doctor Seen:

Reason For Visit:

Treatment Plan:

Medication:

Vaccinations:

Vet Visit Notes

Vet Visit Log

Date   Time

Clinic:

Doctor Seen:

Reason For Visit:

Treatment Plan:

Medication:

Vaccinations:

Vet Visit Notes

Vet Visit Log

Date   Time

Clinic:

Doctor Seen:

Reason For Visit:

Treatment Plan:

Medication:

Vaccinations:

Vet Visit Notes

Vet Visit Log

Date   Time

Clinic:

Doctor Seen:

Reason For Visit:

Treatment Plan:

Medication:

Vaccinations:

Vet Visit Notes

Vet Visit Log

Date   Time

Clinic:

Doctor Seen:

Reason For Visit:

Treatment Plan:

Medication:

Vaccinations:

Vet Visit Notes

Vet Visit Log

Date   Time

Clinic:

Doctor Seen:

Reason For Visit:

Treatment Plan:

Medication:

Vaccinations:

Vet Visit Notes

Vet Visit Log

Date   Time

Clinic:

Doctor Seen:

Reason For Visit:

Treatment Plan:

Medication:

Vaccinations:

Vet Visit Notes

Vet Visit Log

Date   Time

Clinic:

Doctor Seen:

Reason For Visit:

Treatment Plan:

Medication:

Vaccinations:

Vet Visit Notes

Vet Visit Log

Date   Time

Clinic:

Doctor Seen:

Reason For Visit:

Treatment Plan:

Medication:

Vaccinations:

Vet Visit Notes

Vet Visit Log

Date _____ Time _____

Clinic: _____

Doctor Seen: _____

Reason For Visit:

Treatment Plan:

Medication:

Vaccinations:

Vet Visit Notes

Vet Visit Log

Date   Time

Clinic:

Doctor Seen:

Reason For Visit:

Treatment Plan:

Medication:

Vaccinations:

Vet Visit Notes

Vet Visit Log

Date   Time

Clinic:

Doctor Seen:

Reason For Visit:

Treatment Plan:

Medication:

Vaccinations:

Vet Visit Notes

Vet Visit Log

Date   Time

Clinic:

Doctor Seen:

Reason For Visit:

Treatment Plan:

Medication:

Vaccinations:

Vet Visit Notes

Vet Visit Log

Date   Time

Clinic:

Doctor Seen:

Reason For Visit:

Treatment Plan:

Medication:

Vaccinations:

Vet Visit Notes

Vet Visit Log

Date   Time

Clinic:

Doctor Seen:

Reason For Visit:

Treatment Plan:

Medication:

Vaccinations:

Vet Visit Notes

Vet Visit Log

Date   Time

Clinic:

Doctor Seen:

Reason For Visit:

Treatment Plan:

Medication:

Vaccinations:

Vet Visit Notes

Vet Visit Log

Date   Time

Clinic:

Doctor Seen:

Reason For Visit:

Treatment Plan:

Medication:

Vaccinations:

Vet Visit Notes

Vet Visit Log

Date   Time

Clinic:

Doctor Seen:

Reason For Visit:

Treatment Plan:

Medication:

Vaccinations:

Vet Visit Notes

Vet Visit Log

Date   Time

Clinic:

Doctor Seen:

Reason For Visit:

Treatment Plan:

Medication:

Vaccinations:

Vet Visit Notes

Vet Visit Log

Date   Time

Clinic:

Doctor Seen:

Reason For Visit:

Treatment Plan:

Medication:

Vaccinations:

Vet Visit Notes

Vet Visit Log

Date   Time

Clinic:

Doctor Seen:

Reason For Visit:

Treatment Plan:

Medication:

Vaccinations:

Vet Visit Notes

Vet Visit Log

Date   Time

Clinic:

Doctor Seen:

Reason For Visit:

Treatment Plan:

Medication:

Vaccinations:

Vet Visit Notes

Vet Visit Log

Date   Time

Clinic:

Doctor Seen:

Reason For Visit:

Treatment Plan:

Medication:

Vaccinations:

Vet Visit Notes

Vet Visit Log

Date   Time

Clinic:

Doctor Seen:

Reason For Visit:

Treatment Plan:

Medication:

Vaccinations:

Vet Visit Notes

Vet Visit Log

Date   Time

Clinic:

Doctor Seen:

Reason For Visit:

Treatment Plan:

Medication:

Vaccinations:

Vet Visit Notes

Vet Visit Log

Date   Time

Clinic:

Doctor Seen:

Reason For Visit:

Treatment Plan:

Medication:

Vaccinations:

Vet Visit Notes

Vet Visit Log

Date	Time

Clinic:

Doctor Seen:

Reason For Visit:

Treatment Plan:

Medication:

Vaccinations:

Vet Visit Notes

Vet Visit Log

Date   Time

Clinic:

Doctor Seen:

Reason For Visit:

Treatment Plan:

Medication:

Vaccinations:

Vet Visit Notes

Vet Visit Log

Date   Time

Clinic:

Doctor Seen:

Reason For Visit:

Treatment Plan:

Medication:

Vaccinations:

Vet Visit Notes

Vet Visit Log

Date   Time

Clinic:

Doctor Seen:

Reason For Visit:

Treatment Plan:

Medication:

Vaccinations:

Vet Visit Notes

Made in United States
Orlando, FL
01 June 2022

18380832R00055